The
LITTLE BOOK OF
BREATHWORK

T0015932

THE LITTLE BOOK OF BREATHWORK

An Hachette UK Company
www.hachette.co.uk

Vie Books, an imprint of Summersdale Publishers Ltd
Part of Octopus Publishing Group Limited
Carmelite House
50 Victoria Embankment
LONDON
EC4Y 0DZ
UK

www.summersdale.com

Printed and bound in China

ISBN: 978-1-80007-708-9

The
LITTLE BOOK OF
BREATHWORK

Jo Peters

CONTENTS

I AM INHALING.
I AM EXHALING.

Introduction

Hello and welcome to this little book on the big system that is breathwork.

Breathwork is an ancient practice that has been used for centuries to calm, enlighten and clarify the body and mind, but only in recent years have the benefits begun to be more universally acknowledged.

Together, over these pages, we will explore the importance of becoming attuned to your breath and the magical ways in which you can harness its power. We will start to understand the science behind its calming qualities and how you can easily incorporate it into your everyday.

Breathing is the greatest tool in our arsenal to access mindfulness, and you've already been practising it for years. By using this guide, you will be able to deepen your connection to it and watch your full power bloom.

Chapter One

THE POWER OF BREATHWORK

Breathwork is at the centre of many self-care practices, a sign of its fundamental importance to your well-being. It is used as a crucial instrument by the most scientific to the most spiritual of well-being practitioners, as more and more people understand and appreciate its power.

Throughout this chapter, we will begin to look at the multitude of benefits that paying attention to your breath can have, from the physical to the mental to the emotional, as well as the science behind it. We will learn what it actually means to work with your breath, and how you can tailor it to make it work for you. This chapter will lay the foundations for a new mindset in which breathing becomes more than just a functional mechanism and instead a valued asset to help you improve your physical and mental health.

I HAVE THE POWER
TO CHANGE MY
ENTIRE OUTLOOK
WITH A SINGLE
BREATH.

What is breathwork?

The average person breathes in and out 22,000 times per day, and yet how many times have you paid attention to an inhale or exhale today? Most often we only become aware of our breath when it is more of a struggle – when we have a stuffy nose with a cold or are out of breath from exercising. But it is always there, silently whirring away, providing us with the life source that allows us to go about our day.

Breathwork refers to the practice of utilizing these everyday inhalations and exhalations to better our mental and physical health. Sometimes the practice may be as simple as paying attention to the natural rhythm of our breath, and other times it can involve manipulating the breath, such as by deepening it, holding it, increasing its force or using just the nostrils.

Breathwork is simply breathing consciously, with a focus and purpose, through a variety of techniques and exercises.

The aims of breathwork

There are a multitude of reasons why someone might introduce a breathwork practice into their life. While we will cover many of the benefits and purposes of conscious breathing throughout this book, the possibilities are endless and unique to each person.

Because of the many different techniques, the intended outcomes are vast – from helping you fall asleep, to feeling alert and energized, aiding creativity or calming the mind of chatter. But the overarching aim is often the same: using the tools already at our disposal, to clear and focus the body and mind.

Why do we breathe?

Breathing or respiration is the process of getting oxygen into the body and removing carbon dioxide. Oxygen is required by the cells in our bodies in order to perform everyday functions. Moving, eating and thinking all rely on a healthy amount of oxygen being present within our cells. As we breathe in the air around us, we are taking in oxygen.

As the cells perform these tasks, carbon dioxide is produced as a waste product. This needs to be removed from the bloodstream and the body, which happens as we breathe out.

The brain constantly receives signals about the levels of oxygen and carbon dioxide in the body and will change your breathing rate accordingly. For instance, if you are exercising and require more oxygen to your muscles and to remove carbon dioxide at a higher rate, the rhythm of your breath will increase.

How do we breathe?

The parts of the body involved in the breathing process are known collectively as the respiratory system. This includes: the nose, mouth, throat, trachea (windpipe) and lungs.

There are also many muscles involved in respiration. The diaphragm is the main breathing muscle. It is a large sheet of muscle that divides the chest from the abdomen. Many breathwork practices involve feeling or focusing on the diaphragm.

The abdominal muscles and the muscles in between the ribs, the intercostal muscles, also assist with the breathing process.

Inhaling

Here is a basic introduction to what happens when we breathe in:

1. The respiratory centre in the brain signals to the diaphragm and other muscles to begin the process.

2. The diaphragm moves down, and the rib cage pulls up and out. This allows space for the lungs to expand.

3. Air is drawn in, via the nose or mouth, and travels down the trachea, which divides into two airways, travelling into the left and right lung.

4. The airways divide another 15–25 times, eventually becoming thousands of tiny airways leading to air sacs.

5. From these sacs, oxygen passes over into the bloodstream and is carried via the cells to wherever it is needed.

Exhaling

Here is a basic introduction to what happens when we breathe out:

1. Carbon dioxide passes back into the air sacs from the bloodstream.
2. The diaphragm relaxes, returning to a dome position and reducing the space in the lungs. When there is a demand to move air faster, such as during exercise, the abdominal muscles also help to force air back out.
3. This squeezes the air back up the trachea and out of the nose or mouth.

I AM PAUSING.
I AM HERE.
I AM BREATHING.

The science behind breathwork

The body's autonomic nervous system controls all our involuntary functions, like heart rate and digestion. This nervous system is divided into two branches:

Sympathetic nervous system, or "fight or flight" mode

This controls when the body needs to activate a "fight or flight" response in reaction to a perceived danger. When the body is stressed, it exists in this state and might affect involuntary functions, such as raising the heart rate and pausing any processes that aren't urgent.

Parasympathetic nervous system, or "rest and digest" mode

When the body is not under any perceived stress, the "rest and digest" state is activated. This allows the involuntary functions that are less pressing for instant survival to proceed, such as digesting food properly.

Breathing is one involuntary function that can be consciously controlled using breathwork exercises. Therefore, purposefully adjusting your breathing pattern can dictate which nervous system is activated, consequently affecting a whole host of body functions.

When a breathwork exercise involves lengthening an exhale or slowing down the breath, it signals to the brain that the body is not under stress and the parasympathetic nervous system can be activated. During this relaxation response, the body is pulled into a calmer state and can tend to all the vital background functions.

An example of this can often be seen (or heard) during a meditation session, when people's stomachs begin to gurgle as the digestion process is given the green light by their relaxed nervous system.

Physical benefits of breathwork

There are many potential benefits of breathwork. Physical benefits may include:

- Lowered blood pressure
- Relaxed shoulders/chest
- Increased energy
- Boosted immune system
- Improved digestion
- Improved sleep
- Stronger respiratory function
- Reduced feelings of PTSD and past trauma

Emotional benefits of breathwork

Emotional benefits may include:

- Reduced anxiety
- Reduced depression
- Boosted mood
- Increased productivity/focus
- Increased calm
- Increased clarity

Breathwork and other practices

Breathwork is a central pillar of many well-being practices and there is often overlap between them. Because of the multitude of benefits and calming effects, it's no surprise that it is a key part of most wellness journeys.

No holistic venture into wellness is complete without some focus on the breath and its knock-on effects on the whole body and mind. Let's take a look at how breathwork can be incorporated into other practices.

Breathwork and meditation

Meditation is a practice intended to calm, soothe and focus the mind.

As discussed on pages 18–19, controlled breathing can enable the body to slip into the parasympathetic nervous system, the "rest and digest" state. Accessing this state is key to meditating, as it allows the body to slow down and not be on high alert for potential stressors.

When it can feel nearly impossible to simply sit and tell yourself to "be calm and clear the mind", breathwork can offer a focus point to actively pull you into this calmer state. In particular, elongating your exhales helps you to signal to your brain that you are ready to relax.

Breathwork and mindfulness

Mindfulness is the practice of being present. It aims to shift your focus to the here and now, to quieten the brain of chatter and allow you to exist in the present moment.

Since your breath is only occurring in this exact moment – not in the past or future – focusing on your breathing immediately connects you to the present. Every time you focus on an inhale or an exhale, you are shifting your focus to the present and completing an act of mindfulness.

Other ways to be mindful include paying attention to the sounds around you, how your body feels and looking around to really acknowledge what you are seeing.

Breathwork and self-care

Self-care includes a whole host of practices that aim to improve your physical, mental and emotional well-being. This can range from listening to mood-boosting music, having a bath or going for a run.

Breathwork can be an integral part of self-care. For example, for someone trying to reduce anxiety or increase productivity in their morning routine, there are breathing practices for that purpose. Since the aims of breathwork and self-care largely overlap, it's no surprise that breathwork is often involved in self-care moments. The next time you carry out an act of self-care, such as applying a face mask, try to double down on the benefits by also incorporating an appropriate breathwork technique, such as the simple calming exercise explored on pages 58–59.

How to incorporate breathwork into every day

The best thing about breathwork is that it doesn't require any additional tools, complicated equipment or monetary investment. You literally have all you need to get started.

All you need is:
- The knowledge
- The motivation
- The time

Most breathing practices require less than 5 minutes to feel a whole host of benefits. With some, you can even feel the rewards within a minute. While it doesn't require much time at all, you might find it helpful to have set times or specific ways to introduce it into your day.

Here are some examples of ways to introduce a breathwork technique throughout your day:

- When you wake up, before you go about your day, stay in bed a few minutes longer using a breathwork exercise to start your day consciously and calmly.

- Use a mundane everyday activity, such as brushing your teeth or showering as designated time for an appropriate practice.

- Set an alarm for a random time in the day and take a few minutes breathing whenever it goes off, wherever you are.

- Before you eat a meal, use it as an opportunity to pause for a moment and focus on your breath.

- Have a trigger situation that may pop up at random intervals throughout the day, such as every time you stop at a red traffic light or when you receive a text message. Have a go-to breathwork exercise that you can use when these common occurrences arise.

- When falling asleep, use the stillness and quiet to explore a relaxing breathwork practice.

Chapter Two

A BRIEF
HISTORY OF
BREATHWORK

The world of breathwork has only recently begun to gain global prominence throughout wellness and science spheres, despite having its roots in ancient practices that have been used for thousands of years. In this chapter, we will take a brief look at where the idea of breathwork originated, and how it has evolved and grown throughout modern history. Gaining an understanding of how breathwork came to exist and how it has been utilized by humans for so many years, as well as how the practice has been honed for contemporary lives, may help you to appreciate and seek out the many benefits of this wonderful branch of wellness.

WHEN THE BREATH
IS UNSTEADY,
ALL IS UNSTEADY;
WHEN THE BREATH
IS STILL, ALL IS STILL.

Goraksha Shataka

The origins of breathwork practices

What we've come to talk about as breathwork in modern Western culture has its roots in many traditional Eastern religions and cultural practices, and we cannot discuss its current prominence without honouring and acknowledging this history.

Across the next few pages, we will briefly look at how breathing practices are deeply entwined in Buddhism, tai chi and yoga. While these traditional practices, and their work with the breath, are still honoured around the world, they have also been adapted and modernized to suit a contemporary society. But the aims of breathwork within these practices remain the same: to seek calmness and clarity through controlling the breath.

Buddhism

Buddhism is a religion or philosophical tradition that stems from the original teachings of Gautama Buddha between the sixth and fourth centuries BCE in ancient India. Buddhism is currently the world's fourth-largest religion.

Meditation is a key part of Buddhism, and the Buddhist pursuit of liberation and attainment of nirvana. Of the various techniques within Buddhist meditation, arguably one of the most important is *ānāpānasati*. *Ānāpāna*, meaning "inhalation and exhalation", and *sati*, meaning "mindfulness", *ānāpānasati* refers to the mindfulness of breathing.

Ānāpānasati involves paying attention to the breath and is one of Buddha's key teachings. It is described in several of the Buddhist texts or "suttas". One of the suttas in particular, *Ānāpāna Sutta,* recommends the practice of focusing on one's inhales and exhales as a way of cultivating mindfulness in the body and finding release from suffering.

Different branches of Buddhism have evolved *ānāpānasati* practices to have varied techniques. While some put greater focus on the natural rhythm, other schools engage muscles to create more forceful breath and some incorporate breathwork into chanting and singing.

Tai chi

Tai chi is an ancient Chinese martial art that is still practised worldwide for its health benefits. It is founded on the need to maintain the natural balance in all things.

It revolves around meditation and movement, and among its five key elements are *neigong* and *qigong*, both of which prominently feature working with the breath.

A great example of breathwork in tai chi is the exercise known as "crane breathing", which revolves around coordinating breath with body movement. Although crane breathing is for everyone, you might prefer to return to this exercise once you have established your breathwork practice.

Crane breathing

1. Start standing, feet hip-width or wider, distributing the weight evenly between both legs.

2. Keep your centre of gravity low and your knees soft.

3. Breathe in and out through your nose. Listen to the breath as it enters and leaves your body.

4. Place your hands over your lower abdomen. Relax your shoulders and elbows.

5. Move your weight into the front of each foot, then move it back to the back of each foot, while keeping your feet flat on the floor.

6. Develop a steady rhythm and keep listening to your inhales and exhales. Can you link the rocking motion and your breath?

7. Maintain this slow, steady rhythm. Inhale, rock forward. Exhale, rock back.

8. Continue for as many rounds as you like.

Yoga

Yoga is an ancient Indian practice that aims to bring harmony throughout the body, mind and spirit. It has evolved and developed many branches over hundreds of years and is a hugely popular practice for health and relaxation. Whilst the levels of physicality, spirituality and meditation can vary between different schools of yoga, the importance of the breath is a common thread throughout.

In yoga, the practice of focusing on the breath is called "pranayama". In Sanskrit, *prana* means "vital life force", and *yama* means "control". Throughout ancient scriptures and texts such as the Bhagavad Gita and the

Yoga Sutras of Patanjali, pranayama and the controlling of breath is referred to as the key to quietening the mind and gaining higher consciousness.

In more modern practices that often centre around "asanas" (postures), the breath remains a key component. Asanas are often held for a count of breaths, and exhales and inhales are utilized to aid movement and deepen stretches.

We will explore some fundamental pranayama techniques later within the breathwork exercises, starting with yogic breathing on pages 66-68.

The modern rise of breathwork

The breathwork that exists most prominently throughout Western society today is more aligned with the techniques that arose during the 1960s and 1970s. Some were forged from research into states of consciousness and psychedelic effects, whilst others were concentrating more on self-awareness and inner peace.

We will look briefly at the two original branches of modern-day breathwork and how it has developed more recently in the twenty-first century.

BREATHING IS THE GREATEST PLEASURE IN LIFE.

Giovanni Papini

Holotropic breathwork

Holotropic breathwork derives from the meaning of "moving towards wholeness". It was developed in the 1970s by Stan and Christina Grof while working as psychotherapists and conducting research on consciousness and the effects of psychedelic drugs.

Before LSD was classified as an illegal drug, they studied patients under the influence and noticed a particular breathing pattern common among those who were approaching the end of a trip, to prolong the drug's influence. This led the Grofs to research the breath and how it could be controlled to produce non-ordinary states of mind and rapid healing.

The technique of holotropic breathwork involves spending 1–2 hours breathing at an accelerated rate, using the abdominal muscles to forcefully inhale and exhale, often accompanied by music. It has been described as voluntary hyperventilation and can produce a variety of reactions, from laughter and crying to visions and muscular cramps.

While there are claimed therapeutic benefits, it is advisable to do plenty of research and seek medical advice before trying it, especially for anyone with a heart condition or nervous disorder. It should only be carried out under the supervision of a trained holotropic breathwork instructor.

Rebirthing breathwork

Rebirthing arose in the late 1960s–1970s, developed by Dr Leonard Orr, and was also used to heal past traumas.

Dr Orr claims he was inspired by a yogi named Mahavatar Babaji while at his ashram in the Himalayas. Orr was in the bathtub, experimenting with different breathing patterns, when his breath connected with the state of the warm water. The concept of escaping past traumas and the ability to "rebirth" through breath was born.

Spiritual teacher Sondra Ray is also attributed with the rise of rebirthing breathwork after learning from Orr directly and subsequently going on to help others heal from birth traumas through rebirthing.

Rebirthing breathwork focuses on a circular breath, where the inhale and exhale are continuous and connected, in order to elevate you to an altered state where you're processing thoughts, feelings and emotions on a higher level. Unlike holotropic breathing, there is no music involved in rebirthing breathwork, and the focus is on more relaxed, fuller inhales as opposed to forceful exhales.

I AM OPEN TO
WHEREVER THIS
JOURNEY WILL TAKE
ME AND AM GRATEFUL
FOR WHATEVER
IT WILL TEACH ME.

Twenty-first-century breathwork

The popularity of rebirthing and holotropic breathwork practices waned slightly after the 1970s but have found a resurgence in the twenty-first century.

These days, there are dozens of different branches of breathwork, each with its specific pathways and purpose. They may use different stimuli (such as music or incense), they may lean towards group or one-to-one sessions, and they may vary vastly in duration, but all of them involve consciously altering the breathing pattern in order to affect the mind, body or emotional heart.

Chapter Three

BREATHWORK 101

We will now look at how to prepare for your breathwork practice, what to expect and how to adjust it to a comfortable level for you. This chapter will also introduce some simple breathwork practices, which will allow the benefits of breathwork to unfold. These will also lay the foundations for more advanced exercises in the next chapter.

Once you have established an overall grounding in conscious breathing, you can begin to tailor it to work for you and build a knowledge of many techniques to suit different purposes.

INHALE THE FUTURE.
EXHALE THE PAST.

Breathe safely

Before embarking on your breathwork journey, there are a few important considerations to ensure your health and safety.

- If you begin to feel lightheaded, dizzy or short of breath at any point, stop the breathing practice and return to your natural depth and pace of breathing.

- Some breathing practices are not advisable when pregnant or with heart conditions, so seek professional medical advice before attempting.

- If you feel an adverse effect, such as increased anxiety, stop the practice.

- Although the suggestion is often to close your eyes, if this makes you feel claustrophobic, feel free to keep your eyes open and your gaze soft.

General tips for beginners

A few things to bear in mind as you embark on your personal breathwork practice:

- Although many of the exercises can be done anywhere, when first starting out you might find them most beneficial when you can really focus. Try to limit distractions, put your phone away, and settle down somewhere you won't be disturbed.

- Remember that it is perfectly natural for your mind to wander. Have realistic expectations and do not judge yourself if it doesn't feel as easy as you imagine. Remember, even if you only pay attention to one breath throughout your entire practice, that might be one more breath than any other day.

- There is no perfect way to do it. If you feel more comfortable lying down, go for it. If you want to be bolstered by cushions, then do that. Don't be boxed in by an image of what breathwork should look like; it's about how it makes you feel.

- Remember that not all practices will work for you, suit you or be for the purposes you need. This is an overall guide and introduction from which you can cherry-pick what you need.

- Although you have everything at your disposal to practise any time and you may know how good it will make you feel, it still doesn't mean you will always feel motivated. Just as with exercise, sometimes you must force yourself to take that first step.

Breathing through your nose

A lot of the time, when we envision someone taking a deep breath, they inhale through the nose and out through the mouth. While this can be an effective breathing technique, be aware that many breathwork exhales are also performed through the nose. This is more aligned with our natural state of breathing and prevents side effects such as a dry mouth and sore throat.

Therefore, unless otherwise specified in these exercises and techniques throughout the book, always breathe through your nose for both inhales and exhales.

How to begin exercises

Many of these exercises will outline brief advice on how to set up and ease into your practice, often by taking a few moments to settle in and bring your mind up to speed with your body.

As your familiarity with the techniques increases, you will likely discover preferred times of day, locations and set-ups. You may find you prefer to practise breathwork on an empty stomach or that you reap the most rewards when it occurs in the middle of a busy day.

Remember that the purpose of many of these exercises is to cultivate calm and you do not have to be in an already peaceful state to begin. Sometimes you may feel anxious, restless or not in a positive headspace, but that should only encourage you to take a leap and begin your practice.

Noticing your natural breath

The most straightforward introductory breathwork exercise is simply paying attention to your natural breath. By focusing on the breath happening in the present moment, you are completing an act of mindfulness.

This exercise is the perfect one to employ if you are out in public or have limited space, since it is very subtle while instantly grounding you in the moment.

1. Find a quiet, comfortable spot where you will not be disturbed. Close your eyes or allow your focus to glaze over.

2. Tune in to each inhale and exhale, without trying to change them.

3. Notice the pace, the rhythm. Is it fast or slow, constant or varied?

4. Observe the depth of your breath. Is it shallow or do you breathe all the way in and out?

5. Feel where your breath moves you the most. Is it in your belly, your chest, your shoulders?

6. Spend as long as feels good, witnessing your natural breath. If it helps, try to imagine you are creating a full picture of what it feels like to breathe – in your body in this moment – as if you were going to describe it to someone in perfect detail.

Journal prompt

Think of ten words you associate with breathing and write them down here.

....

....

....

....

....

....

....

....

....

....

....

Watch the whole breath

This exercise sounds incredibly simple, but it can be surprisingly tough to maintain concentration.

1. "Watch" or feel your full inhale, from start to finish.
2. "Watch" your full exhale, all the way out.
3. Continue breathing, "watching" the entirety of each breath.

Could you maintain focus for a complete breath cycle?

TOP TIP

Patience is key. Even if the first few cycles feel hard to get through without your mind wandering off, trust that you will get there. Give yourself time to settle into it.

Deepening the breath

This exercise is our first introduction to altering or manipulating the natural breath in the simplest way. We are often told to "take a deep breath", but without true connection to how that feels and what that means, it can be redundant advice. Even deepening the breath ever so slightly will help to calm and ground you.

Have a go at this exercise to begin to understand how to breathe deeper.

1. Start by focusing on your natural breath, noticing the pace and depth of it.
2. Spend a few moments, and a few breath cycles, feeling how your ribcage expands and your chest rises.

3. When you feel ready, begin to gently push past your natural stopping point on your inhales and exhales.

4. Take this expansion slowly; you need only breathe a tiny bit deeper each time.

5. Continue these rounds of controlled, deep breaths until you find a rhythm that feels comfortable yet beyond your natural state.

TOP TIP

With this exercise, try to avoid holding the breath at any point. Keep it flowing at a constant rhythm.

Journal prompt

Describe how you felt before your breathwork practice.
Now describe how you felt after. Was there any change?

....

....

....

....

....

....

....

....

....

....

....

Expanding the breath

Now you have explored how to physically deepen the breath, this can be enhanced through visualization. Using this technique, you may be able to get beyond what you believed to be your deepest breaths.

Visualization is a key tool within breathwork, which often asks us to "see" the breath in certain ways. It is a deeply personal technique and allows you to adapt a practice to whatever works best for your mind and imagination.

In this practice, visualization meets sensation. Can you "send" the breath to different parts of your body simply by focusing on them?

1. Start by lying down, palms facing up and fingers gently spread. Allow your ankles and feet to fall out to the side.

2. Bring your attention to your breath, feeling the gentle rise and fall of your inhales and exhales.

3. Start to visualize your breath flowing into the very centre of your chest, your "heart centre", and filling up your chest on each inhale.

4. With your next inhale, begin to visualize the space that the breath fills, expanding slightly. After a few breaths, perhaps you can see it filling both lungs.

5. With each new inhale start to visualize the breath travelling a little further, reaching down to your belly and up to your throat.

6. Continue this visualization, slowly expanding the reach of your breath, until it travels all the way down your arms and legs. Eventually, your inhales will feel like they are reaching the very tips of your fingers and toes.

Take this practice slowly and notice how the whole body can feel as if it is filled with breath.

Visualizing the breath

This exercise continues to work with visualization, starting to explore with more imaginative possibilities. It is a useful tool for creating a connection with the breath if you are a more visual or creative mind.

1. Close your eyes and focus on your breath.
2. Start to visualize the breath flowing in and out of your body. This could be following the actual respiratory pathways or your own imagined route.
3. Picture the colour of your breath. Imagine your whole body filling with that colour with each inhale.

TOP TIP

Don't get too caught up in the precision of the visualization or worry about having a perfectly formed visual. Allow it to come to you in whatever form.

Counting the breath

Assigning a count to your breath is a key tool in breathwork, whether this is counting each cycle or timing the count of your breath rate.

Using counting is a particularly useful way to focus on your breath if you find it hard to concentrate without your mind becoming distracted. Using a count can help to ground you in your practice.

Later we will explore how counts can be used to lengthen, deepen, or control the breath, but here we simply introduce the idea of counting alongside inhaling and exhaling.

1. Find a quiet moment to zone in to your natural breath. Allow it to be easy and free-flowing.

2. As you inhale, count at a steady pace until you reach the very top of your breath.

3. As you exhale, begin the count again at one, keeping a constant rhythm.

4. Start the count again with each breath in and out and continue for as long as needed to become attuned with your breath.

TOP TIP

Don't let the count dictate the breath. With this exercise, we are simply counting the natural breath, not trying to make it fit to a number.

Yogic breathing

This exercise combines some tools learned so far, including visualization and sending the breath around the body, into a technique that both deepens the breath and heightens concentration.

1. Start by sitting up straight, shoulders relaxed and crown of the head reaching up. You can lean against a wall or chair if that feels more comfortable but try to have length along the torso.

2. Close your eyes and take a moment to connect to your breath.

3. As you inhale, imagine the air flowing directly into your stomach.

4. Imagine it travelling up to your chest.

5. Imagine it travelling up to your throat.

6. Imagine it travelling up to your "third eye" – the space between your brows.

7. As you exhale, imagine the air flowing out from your "third eye", then your throat, then your chest, then your stomach.

8. Continue to cycle the breaths in this way. In through the stomach, chest, throat, third eye. Out through the third eye, throat, chest and stomach.

After this practice, notice how your breath is filling the entirety of your upper body, and how you've sunk into a steady rhythm of deep breathing.

I KNOW WHEN
IT IS TIME TO
LET GO, AND I DO.

Journal prompt

Write down ten things that being able to breathe freely allows you to do.

Connecting the breath and body

Some of the more advanced exercises use physical touch and movements to control the breath and achieve their purpose. This simple exercise aims to introduce you to how you can get beyond just using the respiratory muscles and "mind's eye" (that which you can imagine or visualize) within your practice.

1. This can be done seated or standing, so long as you are comfortable and not distracted.
2. Start by placing a gentle hand, or both hands, on your chest. Follow the rise and fall of your inhalations and exhalations.
3. Move your hand onto your stomach, feeling it expand and contract.
4. Move your hands to your ribcage, observing how it lifts and expands as you inhale, and lowers as you exhale.
5. Now try placing your hands across two areas, such as chest and stomach, to feel how they work in conjunction with one another.

Equal breathing

This exercise is perfect to utilize in moments of high anxiety or stress as it focuses the mind with very little effort. It is also incredibly subtle, so can be done in public without drawing attention. Its strength is in its simplicity.

1. Tune in to your natural breath, then take an exhale all the way out.
2. Inhale steadily for a count of four.
3. Exhale steadily for a count of four.
4. Repeat the cycle, working up to a count that feels comfortable on both the inhale and exhale.

Try this exercise before public speaking or if you feel nervous in a crowded setting, or even to take a breather at your desk.

Resonant breathing

A longer-term positive effect of developing a strong breathwork practice and the ability to control your breathing is lowering your resting heart rate. As you slow your breaths per minute, it lowers your heart rate and blood pressure, leading to a multitude of overall health benefits.

This technique, focusing on lowering the breath rate per minute, directly lowers the heart rate and relaxes the nervous system.

1. Settle into your comfortable position, and tune into your natural breath rate.
2. When you feel ready, exhale all the way out.

3. Inhale for a steady count of five.

4. Exhale for a steady count of five.

5. Adjust the count as you grow more comfortable and relaxed, aiming for anywhere between three to seven full breaths per minute.

This is a useful practice to better your anaerobic stamina, such as when training for endurance sports. In particular, swimmers benefit from resonant breathing since it enhances your ability to slow your breath rate, decreasing the need to breathe out of the water.

Journal prompt

How focused did you feel in your practice today? If your mind wandered, where did it go? Write down your answers here.

BREATHE. LET GO.
AND REMIND YOURSELF THAT THIS VERY MOMENT IS THE ONLY ONE YOU KNOW YOU HAVE FOR SURE.

Oprah Winfrey

Open-mouth exhales

How often do you naturally release a big sigh when you're unwinding from a long day or getting ready to tackle a big task? It's often an involuntary response when our bodies (and minds) need a moment to "let it all out".

This exercise takes advantage of that natural reaction to deliberately cultivate the same sense of relief. Watch how it not only releases pent-up emotional or mental tensions, but how the physical body also relaxes – perhaps from places you were not even aware you were storing tension, such as your jaw, shoulders or belly.

1. Once you have tuned into your natural breath, start to deepen your inhales, inflating your lungs to full capacity and expanding your ribcage and abdomen.

2. As you exhale, sigh out through your mouth. Allow the sigh to be hearty. It can be as loud as feels good and vocalized – whatever sound feels natural.

At first, you might feel too self-conscious to loudly exhale; therefore this exercise is best attempted somewhere you feel comfortable and undisturbed.

Chapter Four

BREATHWORK EXERCISES

Now that you have learned about the science and history behind breathwork, as well as gaining the basic practical foundations, hopefully you feel ready to deepen your practice.

Over this chapter we will explore more advanced techniques and exercises, each with their own unique purpose. These have been divided up by intention and example uses – for instance, for deeper sleep or more energized workouts.

Of course, the prescribed intentions are only offerings and you might find the exercises fulfil a different purpose for you. As you work through the techniques, you will likely determine which suit your body, mind and mood the most.

Remember, the more you practise, the more you will connect with your breath and the quicker you will reap the benefits.

MY BREATH
FILLS UP MY BODY
AND I AM FULL
OF LIFE AND LIGHT.

Counting and timings

The amount of time you spend on a breathwork exercise will differ depending on how much time you have available. Whether you are dedicating half an hour to a full breathwork session or slipping a quick 5 minutes into your busy day, the beauty of this wellness practice is that is very flexible and has something whatever your need.

Therefore, the following exercises do not include a suggested duration or number of cycles. However, you might find it helpful to set a timer or prescribe a set number of rounds for yourself. You can do these as stand-alone practices or complete a few rounds of different exercises as part of the same breathwork session.

TOP TIP

To fully focus on your practice, instead of counting, try to implement a small finger-counting method, such as tapping a finger pad against your thumb to gently keep track without disturbing your practice.

Exercise for sleep

As we've learned, lengthening your exhales helps activate the body's parasympathetic nervous system, the "rest and digest" mode that we need to be in to fall asleep. Therefore, this technique is a perfect tool to help you to slip into a sleepy state.

1. Inhale for a count of four.
2. Exhale for a count of six.
3. Repeat for as long as needed.

TOP TIP

While the counts of this exercise can be adjusted to suit you, if you're using it to fall asleep, avoid exhaling to a depth that's an effort. Choose comfort and consistency over exertion.

Journal prompt

Write down all the things you are grateful for today. Why not start with the ability to breathe?

....

....

....

....

....

....

....

....

....

....

....

Equal triangle breathing

This technique uses a simple visualization, but also introduces holding the breath.

Holding the breath can help deepen your practice, and you will likely become more comfortable with it over time. It should never feel a strain or anxiety-inducing to hold your breath and if it does, drop away from the practice and return to your natural breathing pattern.

1. Close your eyes and picture a triangle with equal sides in your mind's eye.
2. As you inhale for a count of four, follow the line on the triangle in your mind, from the bottom left point to the top point.
3. Hold the breath for a count of four as you travel back down to the bottom right point.

4. As you exhale for four counts, travel along the bottom of the triangle, back to the beginning.

5. Begin the cycle again: in for four, hold for four, out for four, using the visual of the triangle to maintain pace and concentration.

TOP TIP

If you find it hard to envision the triangle in your mind, draw it on a piece of paper and trace it with your finger as you work through the cycles. This can help to maintain focus.

Box breathing

For regaining control

Now you have been introduced to holding the breath, this exercise follows in the same fashion as equal triangle breathing on pages 84–85, only with another count of holding the breath per cycle.

This begins to deepen the breath even further and increase your ability to control it. It can be a great technique to regain mental control if you're feeling overwhelmed or lost. Asserting your ability to take control over your own breath will filter through to your wider mindset.

1. Close your eyes and picture a square.

2. As you inhale for a count of four, follow the line on the square in your mind, from the bottom left corner to the top left corner.

3. Hold the breath for a count of four as you travel along the top of the square.

4. As you exhale, for four counts, follow the square from top right to bottom right.

5. Hold the breath for another count of four as you travel along the bottom of the square, back to the beginning.

6. Begin the cycle again: in for four, hold for four, out for four, hold for four, using the visual of the square to maintain pace and concentration.

TOP TIP

After a count of holding your breath, you may feel inclined to take a sharp inhale or exhale. Try to avoid this. Maintain a consistent flow of air from the beginning to end of a breath. Remember that this is all about control.

Unequal triangle breathing

For relaxation

By combining the techniques of visualizing a pattern and extended exhales, we arrive at unequal triangle breathing.

This method is a more proactive approach to relaxation as it requires concentration and control, but the resulting effect is a strong practice that can break through high levels of anxiety and stress.

1. Close your eyes and picture in your mind an isosceles triangle, where the longest side is the bottom.
2. As you inhale for a count of four, follow the line on the triangle, from the bottom left point to the top point.

3. Hold the breath for a count of four as you travel back down to the bottom right point.

4. As you exhale, for six counts, travel along the bottom of the triangle, back to the beginning.

5. Begin the cycle again: in for four, hold for four, out for six, using the visual of the triangle to maintain pace and concentration.

I am inhaling, I am exhaling

For being present

Breathwork is one of the easiest and most effective ways of becoming present. Each time you focus on a breath, that is you existing in the present moment.

Sometimes it can become so easy to get caught up in thoughts of the past and anticipations about the future, that we forget the reality of the present moment. This exercise is the perfect way to not only practice being present, but to escape any unhelpful worries and be reminded that in this moment, all is OK.

By assigning a mantra to your breath, it helps maintain the mind's focus and become grounded in the here and now.

1. Take a moment to settle into the natural rhythm of your breath.
2. As you inhale, internally say the soothing words, "I am inhaling."
3. As you exhale, internally say, "I am exhaling."
4. Calmly repeat this mantra as you cycle through rounds of breathing.

Remember, the mantra fits to your breath rate rather than vice versa. Don't let the words dictate your breath; instead, they are observant of and commenting on the present moment.

Breathing with words

For mood change

Once you feel comfortable with using a simple mantra alongside your inhales and exhales, you can utilize words to go beyond mindfulness and use them to alter your mood or perspective. This exercise relies on having an openness towards your practice and allowing it to truly settle in your body and transform your mind. It can be used if you find yourself in a headspace that you want to shake off immediately, but also for a more long-term shift in outlook.

1. Close your eyes and take a few moments to observe how you feel, emotionally and mentally. There could be a clear, dominant emotion or it could feel like a more ambiguous mix. Be accepting of whatever comes to mind.

2. When you have a good idea of where you are with this, think about your intention for this session. What thoughts or emotions are not serving you? How would you like to feel in this present moment?

3. Once you have settled on your intention, start to pay attention to your breath. If you haven't already, start to introduce long calming inhalations and exhalations.

4. When you feel ready, begin assigning words to your inhales and exhales according to your intention. Here are some examples:

- "I am breathing in peace. I am breathing out anxiety."

- "I am breathing in strength. I am breathing out fear."

- "I am breathing in positivity. I am breathing out negativity."

- "I am breathing in gratitude. I am breathing out jealousy."

5. Continue until you feel you have achieved your intention, being open to the power of this practice.

TOP TIP

You might find it helpful to use a visualization, such as different colours, to represent the incoming and outgoing emotions.

4-7-8

For release

This technique employs the same sense of release as open-mouth exhales on pages 76–78, however by also introducing a count of holding the breath, it increases the power with which the release comes on the exhale.

It also utilizes a voiced sound to create a force of air as you breathe out. This can be a great way to let go of anger or stress. Imagine exhaling any negative emotions as you produce these forceful exhales.

1. Prepare for your practice in a set-up where you feel mentally and physically comfortable.
2. When you're ready, inhale for a count of four.
3. Hold your breath for a count of seven.

4. As you exhale for a count of eight, create a "whoosh" sound. Try to maintain this sound all the way out, using your abdomen to squeeze out the entirety of the long exhale.

5. Inhale for a count of four.

6. Repeat this cycle for as long as needed.

> If the counts don't quite feel comfortable with your breath capacity, adjust them and slowly build up. Try to keep your inhales half the length of your exhales, with a long-held count in between.

Lion breathing

For confidence

As adults, we often lose our ability to play and be silly. Insecurities take hold as we navigate through life and our place in society, while the fear of judgement can lead us to hold back from being our authentic selves.

This breathwork technique not only has physical benefits, such as activating the vocal cords and releasing tension from the face and jaw, but it also breaks down mental barriers and allows us to feel more confident. It can feel overwhelming at first to step outside your controlled comfort zone, but encourage yourself to take a leap and enjoy a new-found sense of confidence and communication.

1. Find a comfortable seated position.
2. Lean forward slightly, resting your palms on your knees or the floor, with fingers spread wide.

3. Inhale deeply through your nose.

4. Open your mouth wide and stick out your tongue, stretching it down towards your chin.

5. As you exhale strongly, make a "Ha!" sound. Use your abdominal muscles to force out the sound.

6. Take a few natural breaths before completing your next lion's breath.

TOP TIP

The physical benefits of this practice make it great for singers or public speakers. It warms up the vocal cords, stimulates the diaphragm and releases facial tension.

Journal prompt

If you could see your breath, what would it look like?
What colour would it be? Does it change between inhales
and exhales? Write down your findings here.

....

....

....

....

....

....

....

....

....

....

FOR BREATH IS LIFE, SO IF YOU BREATHE WELL, YOU WILL LIVE LONG ON EARTH.

Sanskrit proverb

Breath of fire

For heating up

Hopefully, you feel your level of confidence and control improving around your breathwork. At this point, we can introduce more physical techniques in order to feel even greater and more immediate benefits.

The breath of fire incorporates a mixture of normal inhalations and powerful exhalations, using the abdominal muscles. The quick, physical exhales help to heat the body quickly, which is great when you're in need of revitalization or motivation to get moving.

1. Find a comfortable seated position, with a tall spine.

2. Place one hand gently on your stomach so that you can feel the rise and fall of your breath.

3. Inhale deeply, feeling your stomach expand.

4. Exhale sharply and forcefully through your nose, feeling your abdominal muscles contract. Your exhale should be loud and powerful.

5. Continue this cycle – inhaling passively, exhaling strongly – without pauses between breaths and keeping inhales and exhales of equal length. Repeat a few times, getting comfortable with the practice.

6. When you feel ready, you can speed up the cycles for short bursts.

Remember: Take your time to build up speed and duration of this exercise. If you feel lightheaded at any point, stop the practice and return to your normal breath.

Cooling breath

For cooling off

Just as the breath can be controlled to help ignite our inner fire, it can also be used to cool, both mentally and physically. This is the perfect technique to deploy when you're uncomfortably hot or need a moment to bring your mental and physical temperature down.

1. Find a comfortable position and take a few natural breaths.

2. Roll your tongue, curling the sides into the centre to form a tube. Stick the end of your rolled tongue out between pursed lips. If you can't roll your tongue, purse your lips, forming a small "o" shape. Keep your tongue against the back of your bottom teeth so the cool air can pass over the top.

3. Inhale slowly through your rolled tongue or lips.

4. Close your mouth and exhale through your nose.

5. Continue breathing in these rounds until you have achieved the desired cooling effect.

MY BODY IS MADE
UP OF MILLIONS
OF MIRACLES.
MY BREATH IS
A MAGIC ACT.

Journal prompt

How does your breath feel in this moment? How would you describe to someone how breathing feels in your body? Notice the rhythm, depth and where you feel it most prominently and write down your thoughts here.

Deep breathing

For activity

We often become aware of our breath when we're exercising, as our breath rate increases to try and meet the demands of the muscles requiring more oxygen. It can produce that feeling of a burning chest and panting breath.

This technique helps physically deepen the breath in the body, which makes it ideal to use prior to exercise, to get oxygen pumping round the body, and also after exercise to aid respiratory recovery.

1. Place your hands gently behind your head, with elbows wide.

2. As you inhale, imagine your elbows pulling away from one another, to inflate your chest fully. Breathe in slowly and steadily.

3. Hold the breath for two counts, keeping the elbows outstretched.

4. Gently exhale, trying to keep a controlled flow of air all the way out, relaxing the arms slightly.

5. Repeat these cycles, breathing all the way in, to the very base of the lungs.

Side-to-side breathing

For energizing

This technique combines the breath of fire (pages 100–101) with a physicality that encourages deeper breathing and is super invigorating.

As with the breath of fire, build the speed up slowly with this technique, as the twisting movement combined with rapid breathing can take a while to become comfortable with. Also take care if you have any back or spinal issues.

1. Find a comfortable seated position, with plenty of space around you. Sit up tall.
2. Place the tips of your fingers gently against your temples, with your elbows open wide.

3. As you inhale, gently twist to one side so that one elbow points forwards and one backwards.

4. As you exhale, twist to the other side, breathing out sharply and forcefully.

5. Repeat this, building up speed.

6. After a few rounds, try the exercise again, twisting in the opposite direction when inhaling. This will help you to feel balanced.

Alternate nostril breathing

For balance

Sometimes we feel off-balance without knowing why. This technique can help to identify any imbalance in your breathing, as well as help to resolve it. Once you have gained a physical equilibrium, it can help your mind to feel more balanced too.

The physical requirements of this exercise make it very effective in maintaining concentration on your practice as you have a repeated pattern to draw your focus. If you are sick or congested, alternate nostril breathing will be far less achievable and is not advised.

1. Place your right thumb over your right nostril, and inhale through your left nostril.

2. Release your thumb and place your right ring finger over your left nostril.

3. Exhale through your right nostril.

4. Inhale through your right nostril.

5. Release your ring finger and place your right thumb over your right nostril.

6. Exhale through your left nostril.

7. Begin the cycle again and continue: inhale left, exhale right, inhale right, exhale left.

Some practitioners advise gently placing your right pointer finger and middle finger gently on your "third eye" (the space between your brows), while the thumb and ring finger are in use. You may like to close your eyes and follow your internal gaze up to the "third eye" as well.

I AM THIS BREATH.
I AM THIS MOMENT.

Journal prompt

If you could share one top tip with someone about practising breathwork, what would it be and why?

....

....

....

....

....

....

....

....

....

....

....

....

....

Circular breathing

For releasing toxins

With most meditative breathwork practices, we inhale through the nose; however, with this technique, we inhale through an open mouth to get a greater volume of air into the body.

Try taking a deep inhale through your nose versus a deep inhale through your mouth and see for yourself which one fills the lungs and belly more. In this fashion, both exhaling and inhaling through an open mouth, stale air is evicted from deep in the lungs and fresh breath drawn in.

1. Sit or stand up tall, so that there is plenty of space around your torso.

2. Open your mouth wide and inhale.

3. As you inhale, focus on filling from the bottom of the belly first until it expands out into the ribcage and chest, as if you were filling a container up with liquid.

4. Without pausing, exhale steadily, as if the container was emptying from top to bottom.

5. Repeat these circular breaths, imagining a constant filling and emptying of the container inside your torso.

Humming bee breath

For mental space

Many of us live in a world of constant stimulation. There is always something to watch, listen to or read. Not only can it feel overwhelming, but it can then feel alien to be alone with our thoughts. For instance, with a lot of meditative practices, it feels a struggle to silence the mind because so often it is filled with chatter.

Humming bee breath aims to shut out the outside world and quieten our thoughts by creating an all-consuming sense of "white noise" right inside your head. It is a great practice to use before embarking on quieter breathwork practices, to help clear the mind and tune out unwanted or unhelpful thoughts.

1. Find a place where you will not feel self-conscious or be disturbed.

2. Gently close your eyes and cover your eyelids with your index fingers.

3. Press your thumbs gently down on your tragus (the external cartilage just outside the ear canal) so that they cover the ear holes and mute outside sounds.

4. Take a deep inhalation.

5. Then press your middle fingers over your nostrils – not closing entirely since you will exhale through your nose. Place your ring fingers down on your upper lip and your little fingers upwards on your lower lip, closing the mouth.

6. As you exhale, release a constant humming sound until the end of your breath. You should feel the sound reverberating around your head, creating your own cocoon of sound and darkness.

7. Gently lift your fingers to inhale fully through your nose and repeat.

> If the finger placements don't feel comfortable to you, you can simply close your eyes and press only on the ear cartilage. You can also play with high and low hum sounds, but it should be one constant note for an entire exhale.

Ocean breath

For yoga practice

As discussed on pages 36–37, breathwork or pranayama is a fundamental part of practising yoga, both in a physical asana practice and the more meditative branches. Traditionally, throughout a yoga practice, you should be inhaling and exhaling through the nose, using the sounded *ujjayi* or "ocean breath".

There are many reasons why *ujjayi* breathing is used in yoga:

- By hearing your breath, it allows you to maintain focus on completing full rounds of inhales and exhales, and have a clear idea if your body is under any strain in a posture.

- The physicality of *ujjayi* breathing heats the body, bettering your physical practice.

- If you are attending a class where the instructor may physically adjust your alignment, the sound of the breath enables them to hear when you're exhaling and time their adjustments accordingly.

1. It is easiest to enter the technique by breathing in and out of the mouth.

2. On your exhale, slightly constrict the back of your throat, as if you were fogging up glass. This should not feel like a strain or overly tight. This should create a soft hissing sound.

3. Once you feel comfortable, apply the same gentle throat constriction on your inhalations.

4. The same sound should apply across both inhales and exhales, creating a sound like the tide, hence the name "ocean breath".

5. When you have established this practice, close your mouth and breathe through your nose, with the same throat constriction and the same ocean sound.

6. Use this pranayama technique throughout your practice, until you come to *shavasana* (corpse pose) at the end. Since *ujjayi* breath is used to heat and invigorate, it's not required during the relaxation of *shavasana*.

Journal prompt

What have you found the most effective breathwork technique so far? Why did it resonate with you?

....

....

....

....

....

....

....

....

....

....

....

....

Pursed lip breathing

For shortness of breath

The body's reaction when we are out of breath is to pant by exhaling through an open mouth. It helps cool us down and rid the body of carbon dioxide. This exercise stems from that natural response, using an exhale via the mouth to help slow down the breath rate.

The key to this technique is focusing on controlling your exhale. As difficult as it can feel when you're short of breath, the steadier your exhale, the deeper your inhale will be and the quicker the return to normal breath rate.

1. As you inhale, feel the air passing into your abdomen, not just your chest.

2. As you exhale, purse your lips and exhale slowly, for longer than you inhaled.

3. Continue this cycle until you feel your breath easing into a regular rhythm.

Journal prompt

How has your relationship with your breath changed throughout your breathwork journey?

....

....

....

....

....

....

....

....

....

....

....

Final Word

You should now feel as if you have had a well-rounded introduction to the world of breathwork and experienced for yourself the many benefits it holds and the different purposes it can serve.

Remember that breathwork, like any other practice, requires dedication and exploration to better your ability and discover how it can best serve you. Keep returning to the various techniques and watch how your relationship with them evolves as you hone your ability to control your breath and make it work for you.

With a solid foundation in these breathwork techniques, you can call upon them as often as you need to help soothe, calm, clarify or energize your body and mind.

It is a glorious gift to have the freedom to breathe, so take a deep breath, and go forth into your day with great appreciation for the miracle that is inhaling and exhaling.

Resources

Websites

www.wimhofmethod.com

www.nhs.uk/mental-health/self-help/guides-tools-and-activities/breathing-exercises-for-stress

www.lung.org/lung-health-diseases/wellness/breathing-exercises

www.rebirthingbreathwork.com

www.holotropic.com/holotropic-breathwork/about-holotropic-breathwork

Books

Givens, Jerry *Essential Pranayama: Breathing Techniques for Balance, Healing and Peace* (2020, Rockridge Press)

Granger, Tom *Draw Breath: The Art of Breathing, Mindfulness and Meditation* (2019, Vie)

Kozak, Arnie *The Everything Buddhism Book: A complete introduction to the history, traditions, and beliefs of Buddhism, past and present* (2011, Adams Media)

Nestor, James *Breath: The New Science of a Lost Art* (2021, Penguin Life)

Smart, Andrew *Breathwork: How to Use Your Breath to Change Your Life* (2020, Chronicle Books)

Westmacott-Brown, Nathalia *Breathwork: Use the Power of Breath to Energize Your Body and Focus Your Mind* (2019, DK)

Williams, Edgar *Breathing: An Inspired History* (2021, Reaktion Books)

Wong, Kiew Kit *The Complete Book of Tai Chi Chuan: A Comprehensive Guide to the Principles and Practice* (1996, Thorsons)

THE LITTLE BOOK OF ZEN

Astrid Carvel

Paperback
ISBN: 978-1-80007-197-1

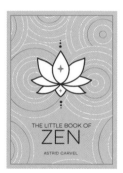

Zen is a philosophy for living in a state of kindness, gratitude and awareness, teaching us to be present and to experience the world as it truly is. This book will guide you through the concept of Zen, revealing how you can apply its principles to your daily life and how you can reap the benefits to gain a greater sense of peace and calm.

THE LITTLE BOOK OF YOGA

Eleanor Hall

Paperback
ISBN: 978-1-78685-280-9

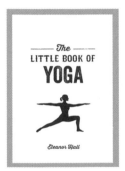

There are plenty of reasons to try yoga – strengthen your body, soothe your soul, reduce stress and many more! This easy-to-digest guide has tips to help you get started and is packed with a variety of poses that target a range of abilities. Be inspired to enjoy all that's best about an awesome yoga lifestyle.

Have you enjoyed this book? If so, find us
on Facebook at **Summersdale Publishers**,
on Twitter at **@Summersdale** and on Instagram and
TikTok at **@summersdalebooks** and get in touch.
We'd love to hear from you!

www.summersdale.com